THE LITTLEST
CORRECTIONAL OFFICER

by Kitty Kesinger Crouse

DORRANCE PUBLISHING CO., INC.
PITTSBURGH, PENNSYLVANIA 15222

Dorrance Publishing Co., Inc.
701 Smithfield Street
Pittsburgh, PA 15222
Visit our website at *www.dorrancebookstore.com*

ISBN: 978-1-4349-2868-9
eISBN: 978-1-4349-2220-5

DEDICATION

To all the correctional officers I've worked with (or trained):
Without you, there would be no story.

Most of all, my family—Dan, Shan, and Kelly: Without you, I
wouldn't be where I am today. I love you dearly.

Transcribed by Judy Settles
"You Will Reach Your Goals"
Typist Ms. Judy: You always kept me going on this book even
when some of the memories were painful.
In special memory of First Sergeant Kenny McGowan: You
always had my back. I will never forget you; you raised me into the
type of officer I am today.

AUTHOR'S NOTES

I was born on June 22, 1949, at Lawrence Memorial Hospital in Kansas, the second daughter of Charles and Inez Kesinger. I weigh only four pounds, with brown eyes and dark brown hair.

There were a total of six of us in our family, consisting of two boys and two girls, and Mom and Dad. Dad was just home from the US Marine Corps after World War II. He met Mom in Hastening Nele, and soon married her.

We took a poor farmer and became dairy farmers. We were so poor but we didn't know it. There was no running water or inside plumbing at all.

Dad works days at a food store and night plowing. It was a hard life. Mom tended a garden for food, canned milk cows, and raised us four kids.

We each had our jobs to do. My brother and I had to pick potatoes, bug off the potato plants, and fried the baby calves.

My older sister had to clean house, prepare meals, babysit our youngest brother, Steve, and keep the laundry wash on a wash tub and wooden wash rock. She would use bars or lye soap to keep our clothes clean.

We went to a one-room school with only twelve students. I was the only one in my class.

One day, our teacher sent us all home early because a cyclone was coming. The three of us ran as fast as we could because we lived quite away from school. When we reached home, the wind was blowing down trees and cows were running wild. Dad yelled for us to get in the storm cellar. He opened the wooden doors and pushed Mom and me in.

Next came my brother, Chuck, then the baby, Steve. The wind blew down our windmill but with it my sister, Jean, was caught flying in the air also.

Just in time, Dad reached up and snatched Jean's hand and both of them were blown down the cellar.

Finally, it got really quiet and Dad pushed both doors open.

Everything was gone: our milk barn, windmill, tractor, car, hay wagons; all our little chickens were dead, the covers were blown and thrown away by trees.

I kept looking for Babe, our work horse, which had brown, black, and white spots.

Finally, he heard me yelling and he came running from under the shed that had blown down on him. How I love Babe!

I now live in McLouth, Kansas. I retired from Kansas State Penitentiary and now work for Community Correction under the United States Marshals Contact. My dad and uncles have all retired and passed away. The only one left is my husband, Dan, who is a maintenance supervisor.

The story I tell is true. I could go on for days about events that went on at Kansas State Pen, but I feel something should be left for another day

CHAPTER ONE

POCKETS

Where do I begin with the life of Pockets? Shall I start at Kansas State Penitentiary, where I received the nickname Pockets?

Should I begin to talk about being a 4'11", 85 pounds female officer in maximum men's security prison? Perhaps I should start the day the inmates tried to rape and murder me, while other inmates jumped in to save my life.

I guess I should start on that August day while waiting for my interview to become a correctional officer at one of the most feared penitentiary in the land, Kansas State Penitentiary (KSP).

I came from a long line of prison workers. My husband, dad, uncle, my husband's uncle, and my son, Kelly, were all state employees. They were facility maintenance supervisors while my husband's uncle was the warden, Mr. Sherman Crouse. I had now opened the doors to be the first female correctional officer of our family to work at KSP.

The interview was uneventful and I was hired on the spot. The next step was six hard weeks of training, firing range, self defense, gas chamber, tracking bloodhounds—test-test-test. We were a class of twenty-one and we all survived the tortures that were upon us. Graduating day was such a high for us all. We weren't just correctional officers, we were a correctional family, keeping close watch on our brothers and sisters' backs. They issued us our "real" correctional officer uniforms that day. How proud we all were. Everyone looked extremely professional in them but me! Being one of the smallest female correctional officers KSP ever hired, they didn't have uniforms that small, so, with help from a friend, we had to take a thirty-inch waist down to twenty-one and inseam from a thirty-four to a twenty-eight.

1

We accomplished this mission with but one problem: The back pockets to my pants were side to side. When I walked down the "streets" in the prison, all you saw behind me was one big pocket. This was where the nickname came from.

My captain would say, "There goes Pockets!" It didn't take long for the inmate grapevine to find that out. They called me that every chance they got.

There is never a dull day in a prison and no two days are ever alike. You must stay in condition yellow—prepare to do what you have to do, alert states, compliancy.

I was assigned the 6:00 A.M. to 2:00 P.M. shift, maximum security men's. I had grown up listening to my dad talk about inmates and the games they play on you, but he would say, "Remember to always treat them fair, firm, and consistent. Never lie to an inmate and be respectful. It's nothing like you see on TV. It's the real deal.

My first test came soon enough the time I was working as second officer in B cell house.

I was at the lockbox in front of the run (a walkway in front of the inmates' cells) waiting for the inmates to come back from chow hall. This cell housed over 350 inmates with only two officers, so the faster you get them locked down, the safer for you.

All at once, the inmates came rushing in from the chow hall. They were on the run calling out a cell number that didn't exist. At this time, I was on the third run trying to figure out what the inmates were doing, when an old white-haired African American inmate stopped at the lockbox. He looked at the run with all those inmates laughing at me, then looked at my confused state of mind.

"You're new, ain't you, gal?" I nodded my head. "And you've been trained not to trust us inmates, right?" Once again, I nodded my head.

Again, he looked at the run, which was still full of inmates. Shaking his head at me, he informed me.

"Open all those cells at once," he said. I told him I was supposed to open only one at a time. He gave me a grin I will never forget, and responded, "I know that's what they teach you all, but those inmates will go in if you do it: my way they figure you know their game now, an' it ain't no fun for them anymore."

I stood there a moment looking up to his eyes and asked him, "But what if they don't live in that cell?"

He laughed and said, "Little missy, now don't you fret on that, 'cause when the man comes back that lives there, I well care of that."

With that, I hit "all select," which opened all the cells on the run; every inmate then went in, just like he said. That old inmate never spoke to me again, but every day, he would come up those stairs and just nod at me and go directly to his cell. I never forgot that inmate. I learned a lot that day. You have to go with your gut feelings in corrections, and not all inmates will want to set you up.

CHAPTER TWO
MY FIRST TEST

Have you ever been so afraid that your mouth goes dry, your legs go weak, you're dizzy-headed, and you really need to use the john? This was what happened to me on my first alarm. I was sent to tower, which was on top of the wall. All at once, I heard this audible tone of three pronounced beeps over my radio!

This meant there was a fight somewhere in the facility; someone needed help, and we were trained if this occurs. You were to take your mini #14 rifle and stand post, arm position on your cat walk (a ledge in front of your tower) until it was announced via radio whether it was secured or false. Looking down my fellow tower office, I followed every move he made. It was only three minutes or less before it was secured, but that was the longest three minutes of my life or so I thought! Another Day at K.S.P.

One day, my captain called and informed me the major wanted to talk to me. If you remember the first time you were sent to the principal's office, that's what it felt like, FEAR OF THE UNKNOWN—"What did I do wrong?"

After arriving at the major's office, he informed me he was putting me in a permanent cell house in max. It was called x pod, five stories up this old red brick building where you could see the town of Leavenworth.

I thought, *Wow, they noticed all the hard work I've done, never missing a day in two years and never refusing a cell house!*

Well, this may have been partially true but the facts were this was called the "aides" cell house—"the death house."

In those days, we were not educated about this disease or precautions; little was known about AIDS. Officers refused to work there, and being the new rookie, I fell for it hook, line, and sinker.

4

Luckily for me, my sergeant was one of the best KSP had to offer. My "real deal" training was just beginning with this hard nose sergeant. My first encounter with my sergeant was very tough, but I sensed a loyal feeling, too. He wasn't that tall, but, pound for pound, he was one of the toughest sergeants I ever worked with; if you had survived his teaching you would become a great correctional officer.

My first day on shift with my sergeant was hard. He proudly told me, "This is my area on the bottom runs. It's called the flag.

"The area about you head is your area. Stay up there, don't come down, and if you make it, I'll see you at 1400 HRS quitting time." I didn't know who I was more intimated by, the sergeant or the inmates.

One thing was for sure: I intended to prove I could hold my own.

I took every word my sergeant said as the color of law: never leave my runs; be alert; keep a 360 surveillance.

As part of my duties, I let inmates out for chow, work, call, medical, library, yard, back in for count, back out for chow again, education call, law library. I could account for my inmates at any given time. That, too, was part of my job. Finally, one day, the sergeant yelled up to me, "Quitting time, bring all your equipment to the office, your relief is here!"

As I came down, my gut was killing me. I hadn't used the ladies room all day, as his orders "Don't come down!" echoed in my mind. Unable to wait any longer, I rushed to get relief, making a dash to the bathroom—but who's in there, my sergeant! I hit the door and asked him to hurry. Not a sound came from the toilet. I hit it again; still no sound. Finally, I said if he didn't hurry, I was using the trash can. All the people in the sergeant office were watching my actions. When the toilet door slowly opened, there stood my sergeant. He had decorated the toilet in pink and purple crepe paper draping like Halloween. Then I read up, "Special correctional officer works in this unit. Keep it clean." To say the least, I was shocked, being the first female to work x pod; not backing gained me respect with these old timers.

TEST #1 PASSED

CHAPTER THREE
AIDS

After we found out more information about AIDS, those inmates who were in late stages were moved to special security hospital.

They moved the ASDO inmates into x pod. ASDO meant administer segregation deputy warden orders.

This meant they were from *seg*, "the hole," and they were high risk inmates! These included such inmates as "the Oklahoma boys," who started the riot in Oklahoma State Penitentiary (Bank Robber Brown, a well-educated man who turned to a life of crime, was among these).

We had high risk escape artist, rapist, and a murderer who, while stoned on drugs, was accused of roasting his son of three months over a gas stove. These inmates were closely monitored because of being threats to the public and the serious nature of their crimes.

I learned fast not to try to find out a man's crime. It's hard enough to deal with felonies, but we are all human and finding out their crime could make one judgmental.

I wasn't allowed to harbor these emotions for they have no place in corrections.

Vacation time was near; my sergeant told me he would be off and I would be the sergeant of the cell house. I stood there staring at him with that deer-in-a-headlight look. He read the panic on my face, but he quickly advised me he knew I could handle it. More importantly, the major had confidence in me.

The first day went fine. I had 144 inmates moving into x pod with little or no conflict.

Day 2-3 went fine; in fact, at this point, my confidence level was increasing rapidly. I was even considering going up for a sergeant position.

Day 5, something went weird in the cell house. I noticed every time I was at my lockbox letting inmates in or walking the runs on security, a black inmate they called "Iron Mike" always checks near me.

They called him Iron Mike because he worked on weights every-day and his body looked like a prizefighter's.

Finally, a light came on. Iron Mike was putting out the message to other inmates, "Don't mess with Officer Crouse." I found out later that my sergeant told Iron Mike, "Don't let anything happen to Crouse while I'm off."

It was a Friday, the last day of acting sergeant position in x pod. Sergeant would be back Monday.

When I walked into x pod cell house that morning at 0603, I noticed the cell house was extremely quiet. The hair was standing up on the back of my neck and I had the gut feeling something wasn't right.

I noticed a sign coming out of cell 110. Inmates often put their cell numbers on cardboard and slide them through the bars if they needed something.

I blew it off for now because it was time to open all the cells for breakfast. I wished I had taken the time to see what that inmate needed.

I unlocked the bottom tier cells, but only three meters. Inmates came out with cycle shank (a shank is a homemade prison knife). Two inmates were trying to kill one inmate. As the cycle shank made contact, blood splattered everywhere. I sounded an alarm, "X pod 1039! X pod 1039!" which meant I needed help ASAP.

I yelled at the inmate to back off and lock down.

Nothing was working. These men were on a killing mission. Two of the inmates ran past me, trying to get out the front cell house door. One was swinging the cycle so hard I felt the breeze as they flew by.

As I ran after them, the front entrance opened. All the responders were arriving to help me, my old pal, Halley, among the first. This kid rode bulls so when he put his shoulder in the inmate, the latter went down. I immediately jumped on the inmate, yelling at him to give me the shank. He kept yelling, "I am going to kill that m—f!"

I kept yelling back, "Not today you ain't! Give me the shank!"

We both fell to the concrete floor. He kept trying to get up as I used pressure points to keep him down. I yelled for somebody to give me some cuffs. A lieutenant handed me a set of cuffs. I and another officer were able to secure him.

The shakedown team was able to secure the other two inmates and took them to *seg*. There were lots of cuts, lots of blood, but no one was dead!

My office worker came up to me and said he held his sign out; he wanted to tell me not to open those cells as there was going to be a fight. Another lesson learned! Each day at Kansas State Penitentiary was a new chapter. School was just beginning.

CHAPTER FOUR

I had been at KSP for five years when I decided it was time to go for sergeant board.

I used every spare moment I had to study. Every policy I could get my hands on, every situation I could come up with, I played the "what if game." I had my sons quiz me on every question any board had ever asked. My time finally came and I felt confident I could accomplish this. I was ready.

The day of my board, my captain came up to me and advised me to watch my sergeant closely. When I asked him why, he responded, "I know he's a dirty sergeant. I want him out of here, you understand." The old time officers had warned me about this captain. If he wanted you gone, you're gone.

As I did my job that day, I didn't notice anything out of the norm with my sergeant.

Finally, I was relieved of duties to go to my sergeant board.

Heading to my sergeant board, again, the captain stopped me and wanted a report on the contraband my sergeant had smuggled in. Blankly, I stared at my captain. When he handed me a cassette tape, I didn't even ask. This was the setup the old timers warned me about.

This tape was full of lies the sergeant had supposedly said.

I told my captain I wasn't setting him up; he then informed me things could be hard on me if I didn't play by the right rules.

Again, I refused and continued to my sergeant board. My board was late because one of the board members was being replaced. I didn't think much about it until I walked into the room.

You could have blown me over with a feather—there sat my captain!

Needless to say, I never made sergeant while that captain was there. All thirty-three times he sat on my board.

After he retired, I went up for first sergeant board only once, and what do you know, I received it. I was the only second correctional officer at KSP to go from corporal to first sergeant. I wore my shield with pride every day. It was a long time coming and I had—and still do have—total respect for what it represents.

After I retired, I was allowed to keep my first sergeant badge. It never leaves me and hard work does bring rewards.

My first cell house was in the medium units 'm' pod. I had been placed on the 10-6 shift of which I fell in love with; night shift was less stressful, and you could learn at a slower pace.

While standing in the main line dining room in the medium, two inmates approached me. They asked if I remembered them. Of course, I did: They helped save my life when inmates tried to rape and murder me in maximum security. They both had paroled out but were back again on new charges. My mind started remembering. Those were dark days in my career at KSP. How I tried to put those days in the back of my mind!

The memory of the pain, the fear, the nightmares, and my poor family, what it put them through came rushing in.

It all started on a Saturday I volunteered to work overtime. Weekends were usually easy, kickback days. Once the inmates were let out for yard, you never saw them again on your shift; "easy money." The sergeant and I were back in the sergeant office, swapping stories, when an inmate came in the office to use the phone on the south side of the cell house because it was quieter there.

The south side had been emptied, awaiting arrival of new inmates on Monday. Each side of the cell house had three floors which could house over 300 inmates. The top cells were for six men to room in; needless to say, it was a high custody cell house.

Correctional officers have to think fast and make good decisions without violating any policy. This is a progression that can't be taught; only by years of experience can this be acquired.

My decision to allow that inmate to use the south phone saved my life. The cell house porter had come to the office asking if I would inspect his work on the top tiers south side. I went with him to check the six-man cell. I stayed on the outside of the cell looking in as I had been trained. Never, never step into a cell with an inmate. A bell started to go off in my head. Unknown to me, this inmate had a history of sexual assaults and batteries. He knew exactly how to lure his victims into his evil web. I told the inmate it looked fine and started to head back down the stairs to the office. All of a sudden, he yelled, "Correctional officer, I need you to check this out!" pointing to the far distance of the six-man cell, and adding, "There's a nail at the end of a broomstick; when correctional officers walk by doing their security checks, inmates will poke it at you." He then stepped out of the cell for me to enter.

As I entered the cell, I felt his weight on my shoulders. I was being choked by his arms across my throat. I felt light–headed; I actually saw little silver stars flickering about.

My worst nightmare was happening: I was being assaulted. He whispered in my ears what he intended to do to me; I fought harder at that point.

I headbutted him to try to get my hand between his arms and my throat, trying to jump up and down to loosen his tight grip around my neck, all the time telling myself, *I have to survive, I have a family that needs me. Keep fighting!* I told myself.

All of a sudden, my feet were off the ground.

It's funny how your life flashed in your mind when you're gasping for air. Seconds seem like hours. With my last breath, I said, "God, help me!" At that moment, I was losing the fight—or was I?

The inmate I had let out for the phone call heard all the commotion and ran up to investigate.

With one jerk, I felt air going back into my lungs. I could feel again. My God, an inmate had just saved my life by yanking another inmate off me. My throat felt like it was on fire. My lungs stung as if a thousand bees penetrated each little section. At least, being in pain meant that I was alive—he hadn't killed me.

There was no time to relax. Immediately, I got the inmate's arms behind him and yelled for help as I marched him down the walk. Officers came running from every area in maximum security to assist me.

At the top of the stairs five stories up, he maneuvered around me and the fight was on again. He pushed, he shoved, he kicked, he threw punches, all the way down the five set of stairs.

Landing on the bottom step, I saw black boots; that meant the good guys were here. Someone gave me cuffs; finally, the nightmare was over—or was it?

Three minutes is a long time when you are fighting for your life!

With the adrenalin rush, I didn't realize I was hurt except for my bruised lungs. After returning from the hospital and going home, it was become apparent I was banged up pretty good; worst yet was my mind.

The same night, my son had a basketball game. We never missed any activity with the boys and I wasn't starting now.

While sitting on the bleachers, my husband setting by me watching every move I made, something weird was happening. I've never felt this way before—it was like having a rerun in my head, going over and over the attack again and again. I could not open my mouth or I would have let out a scream that would have embarrassed my entire family.

Cold sweat was running down my face. I felt I could vomit. Again and again, it kept playing over and over again in my head. I needed help—

CHAPTER FIVE

It was a hot day in May and I was second officer in a cell house. Most of the time, I didn't have problems with the inmates, but today was an exception.

Inmates refused direct orders to lock up. They had a comeback answer for everything I said. They were challenging my authority.

My sergeant was a big man from the islands. He intimidated most inmates because of his size. We became very close throughout the years.

All at once, I felt an arm around me and confronting blue eyes looking down at me.

"I've got ya, kitty; you're safe; want to get home?"

It was my damn husband finally coming down. As they say, my poor family paid the price for years. No one—I mean no one—can come up on my back or I will go into a fight for survival mode.

All the counselors they sent me to could only say, "What's the matter, little girl, can't handle the job?"

Come many a dangerous situation, we backed each other no questions asked.

My sergeant would not tolerate inmates smart-mouth him or his second officers. On this day, even he was having his share of problems.

Finally, as we were letting out for yard time, the inmates were dressed in their heavy coats, caps, and gloves. This was May—it was hot. What were they up to now?

The yard was full that day and most stayed in the "rec shack." This building was a death trap: one door in and one door out, no windows to see what was going on; the tower officer could not see what to shoot at, even if he or she had to.

1400 hours was quitting time; another day. We all walked out together. Shortly, we would find out the 2-10 shift would not be that lucky.

Being at work at 0600 meant you went to bed with the chickens. 4:00 A.M. came rather early and being alert was a must. I was just getting ready for bed when the phone rang.

"KSP Officer Crouse," it said.

The officer told me to report for duty at 4:00 A.M. We had a officer assault on the 2-10 shift, so all shifts were moved up. One thing you never did was ask for more information; if you were intended for it, it would have been given. Soon, we all found out sleep was a luxury we would be doing without.

The phone rang again. "KSP for Supervisor Crouse…." This time, it was informing my husband, a facility maintenance supervisor, to also report to work early.

The news was coming and some of our questions were being addressed. Two Kansas State Penitentiary officers were assaulted on the maximum security *rec* yard. Both were hospitalized under critical condition; prison on lockdown.

We were on alert stage. Who could even think of sleep now? We both packed a "to go" bag. This had the makings of not returning home for a while.

We contacted our children to take care of the livestock, and telling them we loved them. Then, it really hit us. We hugged each other with tears streaming down our checks. We knew once at the prison, we would be going in different directions. Our life would be in serious harm as there was clearly a threat. After the briefing by our captain where we were assigned, we looked and told each other to "be careful and watch your back."

Under no circumstance was any inmate to be allowed out of his cell. Nothing precludes the use of deadly force. If an inmate attempts to give you information, notify the captain office immediately.

Most important, no officer on the cell house runs by himself. Inmates were fed sack lunch, peanut or jelly sandwich, chips, cookies, and fruit.

We soon learned apples and orange being zinged out of cell hitting your head was painful, so no fruit.

Toilet paper fires were thrown from cells. Inmates were flooding their cells, each cell house having each own little riots going.

The warden sent the message to all cell houses water was being turned off to inmate cells and for us to stay in our sergeant office. "Let them live in the mess!"

Hours turn to days, days went to weeks, and inmate informants were giving the investigators what they needed.

The inmates were running out of burnable material. They were becoming tired of living in the foul smelling slop they had made.

Inmates were becoming more personable; the lockdown would continue.

Notification had been given to all offices. A briefing declared Officer Avery was dead. The other officer was upgraded to serious condition. Our captain was given order to reintegrate at high professional standards. We represented the people of Kansas; no attempts were to be made to retaliate against inmates.

The captain couldn't get it out of his mouth before we all walked out and went to our cell houses.

A pound of flesh tastes of blood. They had crossed the line: They killed one of ours.

Every inmate stayed under a blanket in each one's bunk. The grapevine had already delivered them the message, "Officer Avery is dead!"

Main control transmitted at 1200 noon there would be a moment of silence for Officer Avery; not a sound could be heard except for painful moans from officers.

1400 hours had come. They sent us home to shower and get some rest. This act of letting some of us go home was admirable. He knew we wouldn't leave this in any event.

Slowly, information was released of how Mark died: a twenty-five pound-weight was slammed on his skull. We all prayed the first one killed him so he wouldn't suffer.

The second officer was able to crawl under the rec. door. He had been hit with pool balls, pool stick, kicked, jabbed, but he survived. He tried coming back to work, but the incident kept returning to his mind. Twelve inmates were brought to trial; eleven were found guilty. None of the eleven were housed at KSP after the trial. It wouldn't have been in the best interest of security to house them where the incident occurred.

Things started to change at KSP after Mark's death. There was a new glass and metal rec shack where all officers could see inside of the building, an escape hatch for the rec building officers to use.

There were to be no more free weights, no pool tables, extra security on the yard, not all cell houses were permitted go to yard at the same time, no heavy coats or gloves to be worn on the yard, and inmates must have prison IDs on. A new highway on the state property was named Avery Boulevard. It stands there today.

CHAPTER SIX

I had just entered the prison when a sergeant yelled for me to go to "True" unit where we had a "jumper." I went to the location and an inmate I had known was trying to commit suicide. True unit was the special needs unit. The inmate was up three stories going to unit jump; the captain and the associate warden (AW) were standing there looking up at the inmate when I arrived. They both turned to me and asked what I was doing there. I explained I was there to talk the inmate down.

They both turned toward each other and stated they didn't need me, they needed a professional. I felt so embarrassed and worthless. I asked the AW why they had trained me all these years in crisis management if they wouldn't use me. His only reply was, "It looks good."

I turned in my crisis coat, shirts, and equipment that day. I believed in what I was trained to do, but, once again, it was a lesson learned.

I told myself never again was I going to be used in that manner. The warden asked me why I was quilting the team. My only reply was "to ask the AW."

A training officer position was coming to open and I had been asked to apply for it by a first sergeant. "Not me," I said, "I was an old cell house, not a teacher." Still, the persistence continued. I talked it over with my husband and we thought I should have a go at it.

I interviewed for the position and knew it was one of the worst interviews I had ever given. Really, I wasn't all that excited about it anyway.

That night, I got a call from the warden who congratulated me on my new career move as first sergeant and new training officer. What was I gonna tell him, "No"?

I had a lot of knowledge to gain and one weekend to figure it out. I had control of new officers for six weeks. My job was to turn them into professional correctional officer—what have I gotten myself into this time! The first day, I was a nervous wreck. It was a lot different working with my peers instead of standing in front of them giving lessons.

Each class got easier and my people skills became a lot more pronounced.

They allowed me to include different lesson plans, different courses that were within the scope of my duties.

We would have mock trials, with jury selection to sentencing guidelines. We took field trips to state facilities, and visited the death row holding area. This was above my office at Lansing. Many a time, once a correctional officer saw the death chamber, he never returned.

Not all individuals are cut out to work in a prison. My job, besides teaching, was to weed out the ones who couldn't handle it. With weapon qualification, you had to qualify with a .38 caliber gun, #14 rifle, and a shotgun—you had three sets of two attempts to qualify.

If you did not achieve 175 out of 250 on the .38 caliber, 7 out of 10 on the riffle, or 25 out of 35 on the shotgun, you were terminated. Many a person did not make the grade. I expected my correctional officers to be able to handle any situation that may happen by the time six weeks were up.

Every test, they had to achieve 70 percent; every day, there were 6 to 10 handwritten tests. If you failed, you only got one retest.

Graduation Day was special. We had a cook-out, and the families were allowed to come. Awards were issued out to new correctional officers. I felt like a proud parent watching those correctional officers graduate. For six weeks, we worked side by side. I threw everything I had at them. It was not an easy six weeks. When they graduated, they were the best of the best.

Some of my "kids" would even make lieutenant (Lt) and a couple made assistant warden at different facilities.

Inmates and staff alike knew not to jerk around my basic officers; many a staff member was put in their places for it.

The years went by and I had graduated over five hundred correctional officers. I was so proud of them all.

I was now fifty-one and I had spent most of my life in prison. As my mother died at fifty-one of cancer, I thought I should have a complete checkup, just in case.

Everything came back great but the mammogram.

The doctor called and said they needed to do another test; the first one had a lot of ghost in it—whatever that meant. After the results, they set up an appointment with a specialist.

I learned to hate Thursday night late phone calls "from the doctor." It was late afternoon Thursday and a friend and a daughter were visiting when the phone rang; oh, how I wish I hadn't answered it.

It was the doctor informing me it looked liked breast cancer and we needed to set up an appointment immediately.

The air was knocked completely out of me and I yelled at my friend, Linda, to get Dan, my husband. I was in total disarrayed shock. I melted to the floor screaming, "I don't want to die!"

With the phone in my hand while I was still yelling, "This can't be true!" and me totally out of control only confused Dan more.

Taking the phone, he heard Dr. Oply on the line trying to calm me down. My world as I had known it was now totally upside down.

CHAPTER SEVEN

I'm supposed to be a caregiver; that's what my sign, Cancer—the crab—states. How ironic my sign being "cancer."

Our youngest son had just had his first child, a beautiful big eyed girl, only days old.

Our oldest son had three very wonderful children, two boys and a sweet little girl. I was so close to them. I didn't want people to worry about me; this had to be some kind of nightmare. It couldn't be real. I didn't feel sick; in fact, I felt great.

More tests and biopsies confirmed it was breast cancer. The date had been set for surgery for my double mastectomy. The doctors asked if I would sign a release for a special procedure to be done putting a radioactive line in my breast. If it worked, it would show how far the cancer had spread. I was a "lab rat," but if it could help someone else, I would do it. I asked the nurse if it would hurt and she replied, "No."

They sat me in this dentist's-looking chair, pitch dark, except for a multicolored computer screen in front of me.

They then placed this baby chair tray in front of me and instructed me to place both breasts in the double holes and not to move! As I leaned forward to follow their every instructions, I noticed the doctor's silver tray with this monstrous-looking needle and injector rod with this very thin string line attached; *surely*, I thought, *they wasn't using that*.

My oldest son, his wife, and Dan, were waiting in the waiting room for this so-called easy procedure. They were beginning to get worried when they wheeled me out. One look at me and my son yelled, "What did you do to her?"

The nurse replied, "She passed out." As I looked at her, I stated, "You lied to me! That really was painful!"

She said they had to lie or no one would do it.

Now, if that doesn't fill the bill for trust in our medical professionals....

When we were finally alone, my family asked what they did to me. I explained to them after they put me in the adult-looking high chair with tray, they had me lean down so my breasts would slip through these two holes in what looked like a medieval cow ejector; as they threaded the silver line through the machine, they watched the computer.

Up they pumped my chair like a hairdresser. Both technicians were now below me, once again warning me not to move an inch.

All at once, it felt like a knife was inserted through my left breast. I jumped and both techs started yelling, "Don't move!"

I happened to glance at the computer screen and I could see this hose-like object being inserted into my breast, wiggling around like a worm on a hook.

Each time, the tech would push with his medieval injector rod, pain as I never knew got in my breast. My head was spinning. I was seeing double. I informed them both I was going to pass out; the next thing I know, it was over.

My family couldn't believe they did this torture to me with no local painkiller and not telling me the truth. When my husband informed my cancer doctor of this, he was furious with the techs.

Surgery day had arrived. My family was with me as my guard of strength. I would never look the same again if I survived the surgery.

Our little pre-surgical room was full with my family support team. One doctor came in and ordered them to leave. I sat up in bed and stated, "No, they are here until I go in!" He backed off.

They gave me a sedative to calm me and I was in this world of drugs. My oldest son was floating by the ceiling. My husband just laughed, he knew the medication would soon knock me out.

Poor family; they had the hard job of clock watching.

CHAPTER EIGHT

White, white…everything is white…bright white—am I dead? Is this heaven? Where am I? Oh, pain, stronger pain that has pulled me out of so many shadows in my mind.

"Kitty, wake up! Kitty, wake up! Babe, I love you!"

If only I could tell him I felt lost in a deep fog and I was trying to go to his place.

Oh, another sharper pain! Now, I can see him, my sweet, sweet Dan, holding my hand, kissing my forehead.

Finally, I'm waking up.

"Did they get it all, hon?"

"They think so, babe, just try and relax so the pain won't be so bad."

"Did they take both my breasts?"

"Yes, hon, they did, but I love you no matter what. Kitty, that didn't make any difference to me, it's you I love."

When I awoke in my room, my sweet Dan sounded asleep with his head on the side of my bed. I looked pale green. I wondered why.

My room door opened and here came my grandbaby ever so great walking on tippy toes. I hugged Dan and told him we had some company.

Exhausted, he raised his sleepy head with a smile to me and that sexy little wink of his eye.

Our son and his wife asked so softly, "Mom, are you awake?"

I tried to sit up in bed and reply, but I had these strange suction valves attached to my underarms or where my breasts used to be, that is. So much has changed since my last sleep. Who was I? Talking my doctor into going to Texas just days after my surgery was a tough one, but at last, he caved in.

My brother's only son was getting married and we were going to be there, so it had to happen,

Or son and daughter had driven all the way from New Mexico, where he was stationed with the USAF.

CHAPTER NINE

His cousin's wedding, what a fun family gathering! I had Dan stand in front of all the mirrors in the hotel room so I couldn't see what I looked like now. I wasn't ready for that.

After a couple of days, I started feeling bad; too much too soon, so we headed back to Kansas.

All my basic officers, coworkers, and yes—even inmates—had sent cards, flowers, made home-cooked meals. It was really over-whelming. Thursday night, I had another phone call from my doctor. I needed to take radiation started soon. "Just precaution," he said. How I hate those Thursday night phone calls! They're never good!

I went to the bedroom to tell Dan what the doctor had said and had him help me take a shower. Then—I couldn't believe my eyes! I had forgotten about the mirror when I took my blouse off.… What kind of a monster am I? I have never seen anything so gross!

My life—how could they do this to me!

It took a mountain of help for me to go back to work; I was just sure everyone was looking at my chest.

The officers welcomed me back with loving arms. The inmates told me they had prayed for me, and the radiation treatments weren't all that bad. Just when I was starting to adapt to my new body, my administration instructor came into the classroom where I was teaching.

In his hand was a large upper female clear mannequin. He sat it on the desk and said, "What do you all think of First Sergeant Crouse's new body?"

You could have heard a pin drop—I was so embarrassed but I didn't want anyone to know, so I told him to get out and take that stupid mannequin with him.

I should have turned him over the warden, but that wasn't my style. I just went on and chalked it up to his sick sense of humor at my expense.

I found out later the favor would not be returned: he would push for my retirement, my career at KSP/LCF.

Things had quieted down at the prison. We were now called Lansing Correctional Facility. A new breed of inmates was coming from the streets.

We called them generation "Z," the "I want inmate." Mouthier, lazier, believing in only their own needs and not the conduct code, these inmates had no respect for themselves, their families, or the conduct code (do your own time; don't steal from your bunkie; don't mess with the "man"; if you borrow, pay it back).

There was also the problem of "graying in prison" inmates who were sentenced to the "hard forty" were now getting older with major medical issues. The "hard forty" meant you did a flat forty years before any chance of parole. Now, you're seventy years old and have no job, no money; hence, you will probably die in prison.

CHAPTER TEN

The laws were changing, too; more inmates were getting death sentence. Texas was the leader at the timer of enforcing death by lethal injections.

Kansas now had thirteen on death row, with Gary Klopes being number one. He was convicted for killing a Pittsburgh college girl.

He still sits on death row today. The inmates were becoming more aggressive, so we had to make our basic training more intense than it was—not by physical means but outsmarting the offenders.

More females were falling for the inmate con game: "When I get out, we will have a good life together."

More contraband was entering the facility by means of staff for exchange of money. On this one particular day, alarms were sounded because of a major fight in the kitchen. Second responder alarms were sounded.

The fight was a free for all inmates against staff members. Many officers were seriously injured this day but thank God, there were no deaths. Telling inmates your personal business is never a good thing. Getting caught in the dope and money ring can cost you and others lives. A new kitchen supervisor had talked too much about being in debt. Overhearing her conversation, an inmate approached her telling her how to make some easy fast cash. "No one would know, just between us," he would say, but there's no such thing as a secret with inmates.

"The cash would be delivered at a certain location in Leavenworth. There would be a box there. Bring the box to work and just place it on top of the kitchen desk."

First time around the exchange was made, the dope made it in. Too easy. There is, however, never just–a-one-time deal. These inmates would turn their mother in for a sentence reduction.

Second drop was to happen, but the kitchen supervisor decided she deserved more, keeping the money and dope.

The inmates had gotten the supervisor cornered in the kitchen office with only one way in or out. When the kitchen correctional officer rounded the corner doing his security check, he saw the inmates pounding the female supervisor so badly they weren't sure she was still alive. Following his training, he sounded the alarm and tried to render assistance when he got hit.

While other officers were arguing gaining control of the situation, the supervisor was lucky to get out with her life, but she did receive permanent facial abrasions.

Many people think they can work in a prison and come in with that trombone courage from watching too much TV. It takes very special people who can walk in day after day realizing this could be their last day with very little pay.

The public sleeps and enjoys their lives in the free world because these people know their job, and at any minute, will lay down their lives for a coworker.

They laid down their personal lives at the entrance gate to the prison and picked up their professional gear. They don't have the liberty of saying what they want to the inmate, letting their tempers get out of hand, they have to be in control and alert for any and all danger.

CHAPTER ELEVEN

Time again for another health check; each time since the breast cancer, I became a nervous wreck. Never wanting my family or friends to think I'm weak, I kept my mouth shut.

Test was run, blood work taken, and I felt great, full of energy; life was sweet until another Thursday night phone call.

The doctor informed me he had found a cyst on my ovaries. "Here we go again," I told myself. My husband always kept the faith.

A specialist at the K U medical center cancer unit looked at my test.

It's never good when they call you into a dark little room and shut the door. He informed us it indeed was ovarian cancer and growing rapidly. Sugary was the next week and then we would talk more.

Once again, the family was all called in and told at one time. How it hurt me so bad to bring this pain once again to my family. They cried so deeply and felt so helpless; I am blessed with such a wonderful family and friends.

We had started going to the Baptist Church in McLouth, where the pastor was down to earth and everyone welcomed us with open arms. They took us all under there wing

To beat cancer is like fighting for your life against an inmate. Every second counts; you can never, never give up the fight or you will lose.

The prison employees couldn't believe this cancer thing was happening again; they wanted me to take a medical retirement. I wasn't ready to give up the fight. I was declaring war on cancer and God was my strength. I truly believed he had saved me from inmate assaults and breast cancer to lay down now.

There was a plan he had for me and much, much later, I would understand why. Telling my basic officers, coworkers, and friends I would be back in six months, they just gave me that look, believing this time I wouldn't make it. Oh, those of little faith! Once again, our family bonded in the room before surgery. My support teams could not be shaken. How I would draw on their strength in the months to come.

Our kiss was longer and harder this time before surgery. We were both scared but we couldn't let our guard down with the family watching. Both my parents dying of cancer didn't up my odds any. I had been told inmates were actually dropping to their knees praying for me, every day asking how First Sergeant Crouse was. Even get-well cards had reached my mailbox. In the recovery room again, I had the same drill. Dan was by my side, but the words were different.

As I woke up to his kiss and wink, I asked, "Did they get it all?"

He said, "Kitty, they don't know."

Now, it was time to cry and carry on, just Dan and me were there, no guard to keep up. I kept saying, "God, please don't let me die! Please, help me, please!" My first dose of chemo started right after surgery. They were hitting it with everything they had. Finally, I could go home with a chemo port in my chest. We went back home to our trusted old farm, every six weeks I would have a ten-hour treatment. Oh, how sick I would get.

Every morning, I would get up with a handful of hair on my pillow. I looked like a dog with mange. I told my husband I have had enough of this shedding, could he shave it all off.

Outside we went, where there was nothing but the bright moonlight. Off went what was left of my hair. We both started crying. This bald head made it so real.

Our youngest son, who was in the USAF, was coming up from New Mexico with the new granddaughter. I was so afraid I would scare her with my bald head. But there wasn't much I could do. Our oldest son, his wife, and the grandchildren came down. They brought supper and saw my bald head for the first time. They gave me such confidence telling me it didn't look bad at all and acted like it was no big deal. They did me more good than they ever realized.

At last, the new granddaughter had arrived. As our son carried her in the house—she was about six months old—she looked at her dad, looked back at my head, and said, "Pretty!"

I grabbed her out of his arms and held her so tight; another battle won.

The chemo worked and with a lot of prayers, I continued to teach my new basic officers.

I retired from Lansing Correctional Facility with one of the biggest receptions it ever had.

I was so surprised many correctional officers turned out, most of them I had trained.

I have a special place for each one of them in my heart. They were all part of my life. I shall never forget.

Everyone can have a job, but when you've had a career, one with pride and accomplishment, no other job or career can be topped; your heart will always keep it safe—forever.